English Haiku

East meets West – seventeen

syllables – the art of the very

short mindful poem

Written by

Jonathan Wainwright

His thanks go to Liz for her support proof reading, son Ollie for moving to Japan and introducing this beautiful country to him. And to his eldest son, Chris, for his wise intellectual talent.

Contents

Introduction

Haiku is a traditional form of Japanese poetry, typically written about nature.

Pronounced High-Koo, it is derived from the Japanese word Hokku meaning 'Starting verse.'

Traditionally, Haikus comprise 3 lines and are intended to be read in one breath. The first and last lines have 5 syllables and the middle line 7 syllables, hence 17 syllables in all.

However, because the English concept of syllables doesn't exist the same way in the Japanese language, there are subtle differences.

Because Haikus are such short poems, they are usually written about things which are recognisable to the reader and strictly speaking about nature. English Haiku can follow the traditional Japanese rules, but sometimes are less strict, particularly regarding the number of syllables and subject matter.

Chapter One

As the Charlie Nineteen story unfolds, we isolate in fear, ignorance, denial or hope. Tomorrow Britain will be Great again, but the price of that journey may leave us weary, shattered or dead!

The beast is with us

A most beautiful evil

Some die, many don't

Exponential fear

Spreading rapidly unseen

Relentless pathway

Ultimate fear now

Ways beyond comprehension

Is tomorrow lost?

Intimidating

Silver humiliation

A child to be told

Stay in, stay in, now

Such a dilemma to face

Persistent virus

Unseen beauty shows

Across this planet today

Assimilation

Changing our thinking

Such ingenious solutions

Tomorrow is won

Society dazed

Damage not beyond repair

Certainly heaven

Freedom years ahead

Society cares again

New wisdom awaits

Chapter Two

Divide and conquer has always been the politician's weapon. Get the people to fight themselves. Spread fear and 'Fake News' between Nations and unrest will follow. But we don't have to live with this cynicism, or do we?

They are different

But perhaps they are wiser

Now we are fearful

Love Asian cuisine

Unbelievably tasty

Popularity

Liberal freedom

Hate, never far behind fear

Persistent sadness

Escape with nothing

Judged, hated by those they meet

Such cruel people

New thinking means all

Diversity wins the day

Conscientiousness

Kindness wins our thoughts

Loving, supporting, caring

Opportunity

Sharing knowledge now

Thinking in different ways

Can only be good

Build that wall today

They flood our country in droves

Fruit rots on the trees

Taking benefits

Taking resources from us

Caring for Grandpa

Chapter Three

Pitting old versus young is now the new sport

The young are feckless

The old take our resources

No way to live well

We'll educate you

Trap you in a web of debt

Catch you forever

Now, now, now, now, now

Instant gratification

No, save up instead

Whether right or wrong

Youth takes over regardless

Age can never win

Wise from experience

Foundation of ideas

Layer by layer

We loved you Grandpa

Spitfires angels thirty-five

Died for us in war

We loved you Grandma

Green fire engines in the Blitz

Looking after us

Unruly people

Blindingly overbearing

Both the old and young

Today's new humans

Here for the briefest moment

Granite forever

Chapter Four

When we lose loved ones, those we care for, the impact runs deep and long

Wisdom flourishes

Bright talent without knowing

Now helping many

Such a big struggle

You missed Dad every second

Together again

I lay next to you

Gently kissing your temple

Goodbye my dear Dad

Today the earth shook

Conversation rocked my world

But now it's OK

Weariness invades

You fight to remain upright

Gravity prevails

Unbearable pain

Arrives in relentless waves

Inevitably

Let go with kindness

A burden released and free

Then family fights

Death a gift of life

Hearts, lungs, kidneys, pancreas

Yours to give away

Miscarriage, so sad

Death in the womb or stillborn

Tragic silent grief

Chapter Five

Oh the joys of the English weather, a topic of hot discussion despite the pouring rain

Look towards the sky

A conversation starter

Good with a 'Cuppa'

We are all experts

A subject to moan about

The Weather forecast

Why have weather girls?

Don't hear about Weather boys

Unbelievable!

Grey skies up above

Pitter patter, falling rain

Clouds racing across

Crumbly tea biscuits

Special for those inside days

Damp wet soggy rain

Rockers hate the rain

The Met Office Rules OK

That's what the Mods say

Fog, damp dreary fog

Swirling grey darkness again

Good morale boosting?

Fog, smog, pea-souper

Persistent wheezing breathing

Death came the next day

Extreme weather calls

Violent destructive force

Then the calm arrives

Chapter Six

The English do love their Caravan holidays….

It's called a big 'Rig'

The car and 'van together

A Castle on wheels

Know my rights, OK?

In the middle of the road

The huge queue behind

Cheerful times ahead

Good family holiday

Making memories

Perfect companions

Adults, Kids and relations

Arguments galore

Hey, are we there yet?

Mum, Dad, Dad, how long to go?

Terrible journey

Parked by the garage

A big eyesore in the drive

Caravan Man wins

Road hog move over

Righteous in indignation

Forever dawdling

Incredulous names

Buccaneer, Swift and Action

Incredulity

The site is a field

Jammed packed full, muddy and foul

Deep joy forever

Chapter Seven

Tea, a very English institution

Brewed, stewed or builder's

A lifetimes angry debate

How do you like yours?

Tea should be sipped in

Mugs, cups or cups with saucers

'Pinky' finger in the air

A Camomille tea?

Mostly very relaxing

You can hear the scream

In a word, 'English'

A British institution

Yet never grows here

How do you make it?

Is milk first, second or none?

Abominable

Tea leaf or tea bags?

The best way to make your brew

Always wrong for some

Tea bags can pollute

The plastic never breaks down

Oceans groan in pain

Which? Tea or Coffee?

The best drink to start the day

Brought by your lover

Mug, cup, weak or strong

Endless choices amuse you

So what's right or wrong?

Chapter Eight

Rubbish, horrible polluting stuff. Why do people litter, something NOBODY admits to, yet thousands do it, just look at today's roadsides…?

More plastic rubbish

Streams out of a car's window

This isn't my problem

Just thoughtless people

Don't be one of the selfish

Bag it, bin it - NOW!

Airborne plastic bags

Regularly grow on trees

But they never fruit

Recycle your waste

Collected, sorted, graded

Next stop Malaysia

Hypocrisy acts

We are told to meet targets

Rubbish way to win

Micro-plastics kill

Naididae worms, even whales

Your local Ocean

All this packaging

It just isn't needed, is it?

Stop it right away

Lovely diesel stink

Smoke and particulates win

Just go electric

Methane farts away

High up in the atmosphere

Don't blame lovely cows

Chapter Nine

The NHS, a loved institution, staff praised for their altruism, started by Aneurin Bevan, often known as Nye Bevan, in 1946. Where money does not decide whether you receive care

Please get better soon

Doctors and Nurses passion

All they ever want

It's not just a job

And more than a vocation

Nothing quite like it

Your own safety net

Catching a fall to protect

So reassuring

Doctors and Nurses

Scrubs, stethoscope, bones and blood

A little poo too

Life and death arrives

Daily and without warning

Psychological

Syringes, needles

Instruments of pain and gain

You won't feel a thing

I need an organ

A kidney or two kind sir

You died for others

Stuff of hospitals

Outpatients, Inpatients

Forever moving

Ambulance arrives

Speedy saviours to help

Daily life and death

Chapter Ten

Spring, the most beautiful time of the year. Life starts over, fresh green shoots and optimism abound

Looks are deceiving

The Trees only playing dead

Vibrant with new life

Perfect petals

The blossomiest blossom

A new excitement

Shoots poke through the soil

How clever knowing this trick

Looking for the sun

Optimistic News

Refreshed and feeling better

Plants bring us all joy

Time to savour life

Simply under our noses

Such a real treat

Cherry trees blossom

For the briefest speck of time

See it and rejoice

The frogs are mating

Wonderful the joy of Spring

Frogspawn comes alive

Longer days arrive

The warmer days bring pleasure

Special to enjoy

Nature loves humans

Clarity with such beauty

Mankind destroys it

Chapter Eleven

Water; from the seas to rivers, lakes, ponds and rain. It holds life and power and beauty and fascinates us all

The sea looks so calm

Gently lapping at the shore

The next day angry

Violence unleashed

The Tornado's path strikes fear

Random destruction

Cascading water

Dripping off the mountain side

Forever flowing

Reflections ripple

The picture is upside down

It makes not a sound

Blue grey sky above

Churning shingle, sand and life

The storm has arrived

Travelling the cut

The narrowboats slow progress

A wonderful world

Puddles all around

Children wearing rubber boots

Slash, splash, splash, get wet

Violent rain falls

A tumbling, massive wetness

That spreads and destroys

From mist to drizzle

Grey elegant depression

Comes with the damp too

Chapter Twelve

Narrowboating on the UK canals, a real treat. Life sloooows down, so you really experience the world around you. Travel through country, city and town. World's best kept secret - don't tell anyone

Work is the new play

Chug, chug, chug, slowly does it

Victorians rule

A special journey

Viaduct, aqueduct, bridge

Only on the cut

From short to long boats

All of them six foot ten wide

Else get stuck in locks

They made the canals

Telford, Smeaton and Brindley

Amazing talent

Such a treat to see

Blue flash of the kingfisher

Takes your breath away

Up and down a lock

Half a million gallons flow

So share with a friend

The canal side pub

A fine tale and pint enjoyed

To slake the day's work

You are going too fast!

Please slowdown past my mooring

It just rocks my world

Hirer or owner

The water is shared by all

But know your station

Chapter Thirteen

Work, love it or hate it as well as providing income it shapes our lives for better or worse…. the pain of interviews, bosses, customers and colleagues

The job didn't happen

Aaaagh, very annoying

How the lion roars

Awkward pregnant pause

Fine debate, no chemistry

The job won't happen

Interview went wrong

Then we found a common thread

Boom. Start tomorrow

Waiting for an hour

This is shameful power play

Always the same thing

Meetings, more meetings

Nothing is solved, rambling on

Life leaking away

My lovely work mates

What a joy when they help me

They make it worthwhile

The five o'clock call

Always comes on a Friday

"I need it Monday"

Customer is king

Yeah right, what about workers?

Who helps pay the bills?

What's work life balance?

Really Management speak

Work you to the bone

Chapter Fourteen

Fear is a terrible thing to deal with. We can't all be SAS heroes, but we need to master this emotion

Who dares sometimes wins

Stirring us into action

Imagination

The dry mouth shiver

Makes us shake, keeps us alert

One step at a time

Fear comes in the night

The small wee hours of wild thought

Please just get a grip

The bully looms big

Finding weakness to prey on

Be smarter than that

Fear is not constant

Wave after wave after wave

Will never break me

Fear - a friend or foe

A little bit sharpens things

Much traumatises

Heros look for it

To become fearless and brave

A rare quality

We all hate cowards

We all worship a hero

The difference - fear

Be so very strong

With courage cast fear aside

Dubious pleasure

Chapter Fifteen

When we reach a crossroads in our lives we can either go forward into the future with confidence, looking forward to new challenges, or be daunted by the whole process and overcome

Today I'm reborn

Now fresh, new, clear of the past

Free to find my way

The pain of great loss

A relentless crushing weight

Chuck it off a cliff

So completely lost

Now I don't know what to do

My scream just isn't heard

Left, right, back, forward

Which is the best way to turn?

Just be brave, go now

A leap of true faith

Daunting yet easy to do

Overthinking kills

Think, a year from now

Moving on feels hard to do

It really isn't

Mood swings back and forth

Good, bad and indifferent

Which feeling is right?

A beautiful change

Truly wonderful feeling

Unbelievable

What a difference

A brand new life to enjoy

A priceless moment

Chapter Sixteen

For twenty-five years my passion was flying light aircraft. One day, after over 700 hours flying time, it left me, so at 13.20 on the 17th December 2012, I just stopped. I haven't looked back

My instructor's gone

First solo is such a thrill

Lifeline's gone now

What an irony

Summer haze can spoil the view

High pressure build up

Rules with no freedom

More and more controlled airspace

No longer welcome

Bonjour Le Touquet

Flight plan filed, life jackets on

Real achievement

From Snoring to Sleap

Favourite logbook entry

Only an hour's flight

Fluffy Cumulus

Beautiful fair weather clouds

When they tower, help!

Takeoffs and Landings

The same number of each, please

Otherwise you die

Freedom in the air

The land unfolds underneath

Just get lost in time

Flying sometimes bites

So Gambolling not Gambling

Ignore at peril

Chapter Seventeen

We take clouds for granted, silently floating above us. Yet without them we would perish as they are the giver of life, bringing precious water to make the land fertile and crops grow

Prowling Cumulous

Fair weather or foul they grow

Anvil headed spite

Fluffy little cloud

White gold moving above us

Their rain saves our life

Stratus grey blanket

Makes a sky like depression

And drizzle to please

Rare Lenticular

Exciting, spooky and strange

Designed by Gaudi

A hidden wonder

Thunder, lightning rain and wind

Epic electrons

Silently building

Front moving ever nearer

Takes the sun away

Blue skies, gentle breeze

Makes us feel alive right now

Always Remember

Very clever clouds

Rain, hail, drizzle, mist and snow

Special orchestra

Excited children

They never tire of moving

Ever stealthily

Chapter Eighteen

Flowers fill our lives with beautiful colours, shapes and smells to delight our senses. What would we do without them?

Simply wonderful

Only if our eyes can see

Breathtaking delight

Pesticides rain down

Vibrant colours in their path

A sad wasteful death

Symbols of valour

Blood red poppies all around

Indelible waste

Bringing joy to us

Just an exquisite beauty

To tease and delight

Such a short, short life

A couple of weeks at best

Perfect forever

Angels in the breeze

Swaying in time with the bees

Generosity

Huge, big, small, tiny

All shapes, size, colours and smell

Never ending choice

Boring little seeds

They can come in a packet

Grow into treasure

Lonely small flower

Beauty in their huge numbers

A magic carpet

Chapter Nineteen

War fills our hearts with terror, yet humankind constantly fights - how deeply wrong that the innocent always suffer most. There must be a better way?

The words avoided

Sanitised killing OK?

euphemisms galore

Young men die so young

Generations blown away

Needless bloody waste

Shattered Syria

A beauty smashed to pieces

Civilisation?

Who really wins

Leaders just 'Willy Wave'

People pay the price

Mind focusing war

Awesome ingenuity

Can't even cure colds

People die badly

Or collateral damage

It sounds comforting

Glorify the dead

Remember their sacrifice

The living as well

Injured forever

Physical and mental scars

Rubbish tossed aside

Brilliant smart weapons

Ultimate killing machine

Highly directed

Chapter Twenty

Cars have revolutionised personal transport, nothing comes close. Yet this convenience will soon be outweighed by the inconvenience of traffic jams and pollution

Whichever you choose

Electric, diesel or gas

Jams always prevail

All do the same job

Shiny, dirty or rusty

No, my car is me

So many car brands

Prestige or for the people

Just implausible

Reality shows

Top and Fifth Gear, now Grand Tour

Car programme to dull?

Fines for this and that

But never for the other

Thanks, passive income

Murder with a knife

An accident with a car

Thousands every year

We love motorsport

Touring, Indy and F1 cars

Go round in circles

A new love affair

Lavish cars with affection

Don't forget the wives

Red, silver and gold

Drooling and sparkling magic

The colour of lust

Chapter Twenty-One

I admire birds and what these industrious little bundles of energy can achieve. Just how do they fly and navigate thousands of miles, and with a weight in grams, deal with the weather?

Stop right this second

His bright red breast all puffed up

Robin fears no one

Gull whizzing around

You 'Gotta Chip', 'Gotta Chip'

No rest eating here

So Electric blue

Fighting with such bright orange

Speedy Kingfisher

Patiently stands still

For hours and hours all alone

Heron strikes a fish

Big busy pigeon

Crap dashes a tourist's head

All over the place

Wobble, wobble way

A wagtail's humourous strut

Very amusing

Hovering high up

Looking down below for prey

Hawked into road kill

Stupid pheasant struts

Gives kerb life up for a car

Elegant yet dim

Eating fresh earthworms

Blackbird stay in my garden

A seductive song

Chapter Twenty-Two

I love the Advertising Agency world. It is full of characters and passion. Key was always winning the new business pitch, that and matching business, staff and income was a key driver. And the very personalities that made it, also pulled it apart

Art directors rule

Brave creative ideas

Markers of iron

Herding sleeping sheep

Just let planners plan instead

Infogram alert

Pitch team meets to plan

Egos easily collide

A new axe to grind

Why Action Stations?

Client visits agency

Is that the budget?

Strategy is all

Grind ideas to the bone

Only right answers

Research is godlike

Does it answer the question?

skilfully argued

Thought leaders arise

Dubbing the right solution

With the right angle?

Far too much at stake

It's a serious business

Money talks loudest

Digital's a dream

New science meets old snake oil

Clever way to spin

Chapter Twenty-Three

Despite the Government's best endeavours, Charlie Nineteen and lockdown has turned the small business world upside down. Will these companies survive and how? What future, if any, awaits them? Only questions right now, no answers in sight at all. Nothing, nadaa

Right out of the blue

shutdown tight, Pause button on

Think, where do I start?

Will banks support me?

Will suppliers still be there?

Bank account empty

Debtors can't pay me

Charlie cash flow is not king

Lack of sympathy

Loyal staff for years

Furloughed for weeks maybe months

Work again someday?

Try a new car sir?

It has a Charlie filter

NCAP safety tested!

Working from home now

No customers to talk to

Redundant, useless

Chin up young people

Keep your positivity

Could have been Brexit

Balancing high wire

Will the workers left get sick?

Clowns laugh and cry tears

We are nearly done

Not in my reality

Let's get creative

Thank you for taking the time to read my Haiku.
I hope that you have enjoyed them and that they have resonated with
your life experiences.

Jonathan Wainwright

english.haiku@gmail.com

Printed in Great Britain
by Amazon

84668741R00048